WHY SHOULD I WASH MY HAIR?

✦ and other questions about healthy skin

and hair ✦

Heinemann
LIBRARY

Louise Spilsbury

www.heinemann.co.uk/library
Visit our website to find out more information about **Heinemann Library** books.

To order:
 Phone 44 (0) 1865 888066
 Send a fax to 44 (0) 1865 314091
 Visit the Heinemann Bookshop at www.heinemann.co.uk/library to browse our catalogue and order online.

First published in Great Britain by Heinemann Library, Halley Court, Jordan Hill, Oxford OX2 8EJ, part of Harcourt Education.
Heinemann is a registered trademark of Harcourt Education Ltd.

Editorial: Nancy Dickmann, Jennifer Tubbs and Louise Galpine
Design: David Poole and Tokay Interactive Ltd (www.tokay.co.uk)
Illustrations: Kamae Design Ltd
Picture Research: Rebecca Sodergren and Liz Eddison
Production: Séverine Ribierre and Jonathan Smith

Originated by Ambassador Litho Ltd
Printed in China by Wing King Tong

ISBN 0 431 11096 4
07 06 05 04 03
10 9 8 7 6 5 4 3 2 1

British Library Cataloguing in Publication Data
Spilsbury, Louise
Why Should I Wash my Hair? and other questions about healthy skin and hair
612.7'9
A full catalogue record for this book is available from the British Library.

Acknowledgements
Bubbles pp. **13** (Jennie Woodcock), **22** (Angela Hampton); Corbis pp. **20** (Nancy Nev), **25** (Paul A Souders), **27** (Lester V Bergman); Getty Images pp. **4**, **8**, **24** (Taxi) **7**, **23** (Imagebank); Liz Eddison p. **16**; Science Photo Library pp. **5**, **14**, **18**, **19**, **26**; Tudor Photography pp. **10**, **11**, **12**, **15**, **17**, **21**, **28**.

Cover photograph of child washing hair, reproduced with permission of Tudor Photography.

The publishers would like to thank Julie Johnson for her assistance in the preparation of this book.

Every effort has been made to contact copyright holders of any material reproduced in this book. Any omissions will be rectified in subsequent printings if notice is given to the publishers.

CONTENTS

Words appearing in the text in bold, **like this**, are explained in the Glossary.

WHY IS HEALTHY SKIN IMPORTANT?

Most of us do not think of our skin as having much to do – it just covers our bodies. In fact, skin is a vitally important body part, like your heart or brain, and you should take care of it.

Skin protection

Skin is like your body's armour. It may feel soft, but skin works very hard, protecting your insides from dirt and dust, bumps and knocks, wind and rain, and **germs**. Although germs can get into your body through your mouth and nose, the only way they can get through your skin is if you have a cut in it.

Your skin is also like a waterproof coat – it stops water getting into and out of your body. The organs inside your body need just the right amount of moisture to work well. Your skin stops them from getting too wet or too dry.

Hot and cold

Your skin helps to keep your body at a healthy temperature. On a cold day, the hairs on your body stand up, trapping a layer of warm air around you. Small **blood vessels** under the skin, called capillaries, get thinner, to keep them away from the skin's surface so they can hold on to their warmth. When it is hot, the hairs lie flat, and the capillaries bring warm blood to the skin's surface, to release some of their heat.

A touchy subject?

Your skin also provides you with your sense of touch. It lets you feel whether something is hard or soft, or hot or cold. There are **nerve endings** just beneath the surface of your skin, which send messages to your brain about everything that you touch.

When the hair on your skin stands up to trap warmth, we call it 'goosebumps'.

How does skin work?

Your skin is made up of three layers. The outside layer – the **epidermis** – is always changing. New **cells** made at the bottom slowly work their way to the top, filling in with a tough substance called **keratin** as they go. They die as they reach the top and form the skin's surface.

The middle layer – the dermis – contains **nerve endings**, **blood vessels** and **glands**. Blood vessels bring food and **oxygen** to the cells. Glands make oil and sweat.

The bottom – subcutaneous – layer is mostly fat. It helps to keep you warm and acts like a cushion, absorbing the shock when you knock your skin.

Your skin is not as simple as it looks!

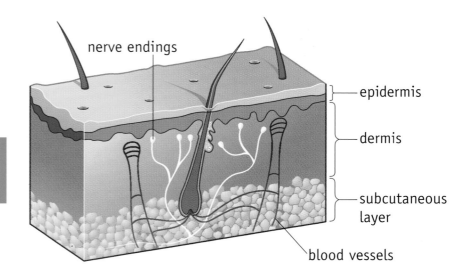

nerve endings

epidermis

dermis

subcutaneous layer

blood vessels

WHY SHOULD I CARE FOR MY HAIR?

You should take care of the hair on your head because it has a very important job to do. It helps to keep your brain at a steady temperature. The brain is one of the most important parts in your body – it controls everything you think, feel and do – and it needs to be at a steady temperature to work at its best.

On a cold day, your hair keeps your head warm. On a hot day, it protects your head from some of the Sun's heat. Your hair also provides some cushioning when you bump your head, helping to prevent your brain being hurt.

Your hair is also important because it is a part of who you are. If you are asked to describe someone, the chances are that one of the first things you will describe is their hair colour and style.

SKIN AND HAIR COLOUR

The colour of a person's skin is often linked to the colour of their hair, because skin and hair colour are decided by the amount of melanin a person makes. People with blonde or red hair make less melanin, so they also have light skin. People with dark skin make more melanin, so they usually have dark hair.

Why do people have different coloured hair?

The thing that decides whether you have blonde, brown, red or black hair is the amount of **melanin** your body makes. Melanin is a substance that colours skin and hair. **Cells** in the **epidermis** make melanin. They colour hair as it grows. The more melanin you make, the darker your hair is. As you get older, you make less melanin. That is why elderly people have grey or white hair.

You **inherit** the kind of hair you have from your parents.

How does hair grow?

You have some hair all over your body, and all of it grows in the same way – from a root. A root is a patch of cells that form **keratin**, a substance that makes your hair strong. Each root is inside a **follicle** and, at the bottom of the follicles, there are tiny **blood vessels** that supply the hair root with food.

The root is the only part of a hair that is alive. It makes a strand of hair grow out of a **pore** (tiny hole) in the skin. The hair that you can see is dead. It is made up of dead cells of keratin. After a while, the strand of hair falls out, and the root makes a new one to replace it.

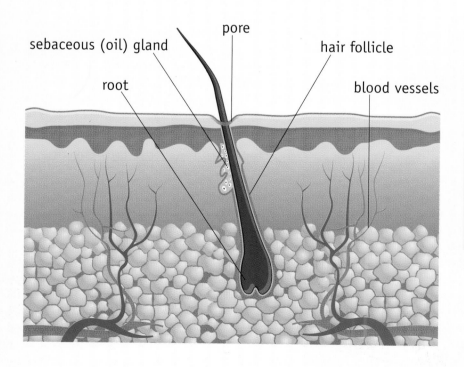

sebaceous (oil) gland

pore

hair follicle

root

blood vessels

Near each hair follicle is a **sebaceous gland**, which makes a kind of oil called sebum. This oil helps to make your hair shine, and also makes it a bit waterproof.

If you have long hair that you tie back, one thing you can do to look after your hair is to avoid wearing thin elastic bands. Scrunchies, like this, are less likely to break strands of hair.

What makes hair curly?

The type of hair you have – whether it is curly or straight, thick or fine – depends on your **follicles**. If you have large hair follicles, you are likely to have thick hair. If your follicles are small, your hair will be fine. Oval follicles make wavy hair, round follicles make straight hair and flat follicles make curly hair.

Why do I need a haircut?

One reason people get their hair cut is because they like to have a particular hairstyle. Regular trimming also gets rid of split ends. Split ends – when the end of a strand of hair splits into two – happens when the outer layer of a hair, called the **cuticle**, is damaged.

WHY SHOULD I TAKE A SHOWER OR BATH?

You need to take showers or baths because a vital part of taking care of your skin is keeping it clean. One of your skin's most important jobs is to protect your insides from **germs**. You need to help your skin to do its job by washing off dust, dirt and stale sweat, which can carry germs.

What is sweat?

When you get hot, your sweat **glands** make sweat – a kind of salty water. The sweat leaves your body through tiny holes in your skin, called **pores**. As sweat dries in the air, it cools you down. Some sweat stays on your skin, and **bacteria** start to grow on it. This is what makes sweat smell. If these bacteria get into your body, they can make you ill.

When you wash, you also rub off the old, dead skin **cells** that build up on your skin's surface.

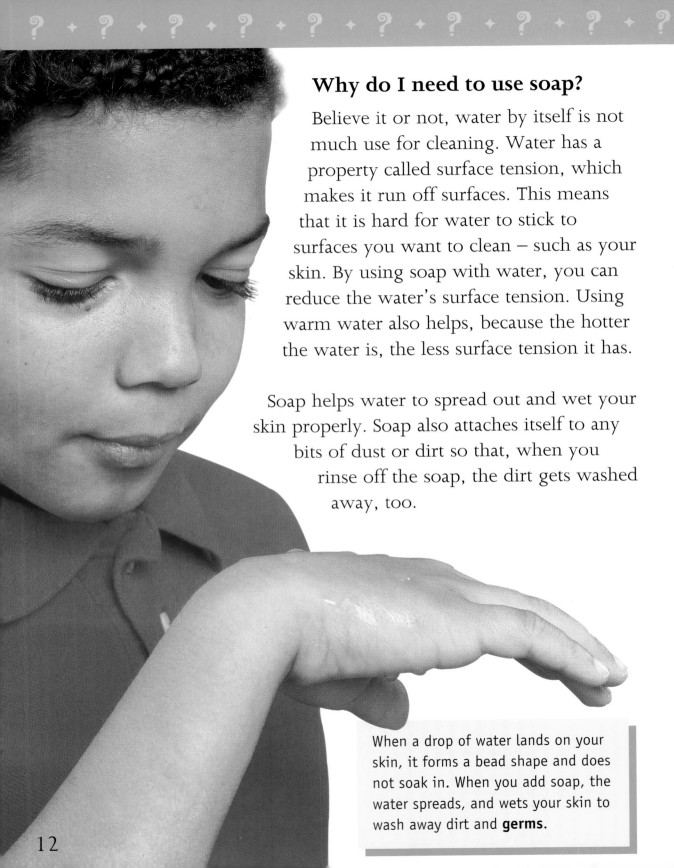

Why do I need to use soap?

Believe it or not, water by itself is not much use for cleaning. Water has a property called surface tension, which makes it run off surfaces. This means that it is hard for water to stick to surfaces you want to clean – such as your skin. By using soap with water, you can reduce the water's surface tension. Using warm water also helps, because the hotter the water is, the less surface tension it has.

Soap helps water to spread out and wet your skin properly. Soap also attaches itself to any bits of dust or dirt so that, when you rinse off the soap, the dirt gets washed away, too.

When a drop of water lands on your skin, it forms a bead shape and does not soak in. When you add soap, the water spreads, and wets your skin to wash away dirt and **germs**.

What soap should I use?

For most people, it does not matter what kind of soap they use. If you have sensitive skin — skin that is easily irritated by things — you should avoid soaps that have a lot of perfume in them. Try to buy pure soaps or those that are specially designed for people with sensitive skin.

WAYS OF WASHING

Do not use water that is very hot when you take a shower or bath, because it can scald (burn) your skin. Cold water does not clean well, so use warm water. Germs thrive in damp places, so dry yourself thoroughly with a clean towel after washing. Dry between your toes, too – this helps to prevent **athlete's foot.**

Showers are a good way to wash, because you can rinse off dirt more easily. Showers also use less water than baths, and it is good to save water when you can.

WHY SHOULD I WASH MY HAIR?

There are no hard and fast rules about washing your hair. Most young people wash their hair about once a week, or when it feels dirty. You need to wash it more often if you do a lot of sport, or if it is very hot and you sweat a lot.

Why does my hair need washing?

You need to wash your hair to keep it clean. Some people find that their hair feels greasy when it needs a wash, because their **sebaceous glands** have made too much oil. Dirt and dust collect on your hair, just as they do on your clothes and skin, so you need to wash those off, too.

This picture shows a hair coming out of a **scalp**. At the bottom of each strand, you can see dead skin **cells**, which look like flakes. When you wash your hair, you wash these off.

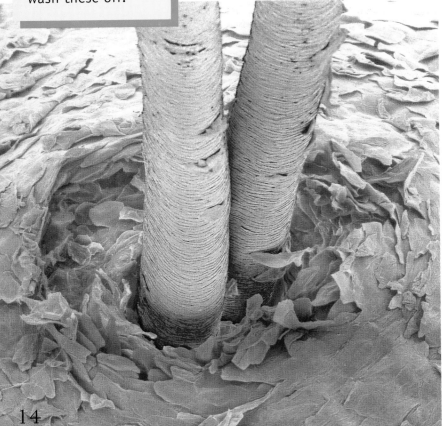

Can you wash hair too often?

Although it is good to wash your hair regularly, it is bad to wash it too often. When you use shampoo, you also wash off some of the natural oils that your skin produces to coat your hair as it grows. These oils are important, because they keep the strands of hair supple and waterproof.

WHY WASH HAIR AFTER SWIMMING?

You should always wash your hair after swimming, to protect it. Swimming pools contain chemicals, such as chlorine, that can burn your hair if they stay on it for too long. Sea water is salty and it dries your hair out, so make sure that you wash it out of your hair after a day at the beach.

When you wash your hair, use warm water and rub the shampoo in with your fingertips. Rinse your hair with clean water to get out all the shampoo.

Some people prefer to use 'natural' shampoos. These are usually made from plants, and do not contain the strong chemicals that some ordinary shampoos contain.

Why use shampoo?

Most people use shampoo to wash their hair for the same reason that they use soap to wash their skin. Because of surface tension, water is not very good at wetting or cleaning when used on its own. The oily layer on your hair is slightly waterproof, so the water just runs off it. The **detergents** in shampoo attach to the dirt and flakes of dead **cells** on your hair, so that, when you rinse it, they wash away down the plughole with the water.

WHAT IS IN SHAMPOO?

Most shampoos contain: water, substances called foaming agents, which make bubbles when the shampoo is mixed with water, detergents to clean the hair, and perfumes to cover up the smell of the detergents!

Which shampoo should I use?

Try to use a shampoo that says 'mild' or 'gentle' on the label. Strong shampoos may contain more chemicals, which can damage your hair. If your hair feels greasy, you may need to use a shampoo especially for oily or greasy hair.

What is conditioner?

People sometimes use conditioner after they have washed their hair with shampoo. You usually spread a small amount of conditioner on to your hair, leave it for a minute and then rinse it thoroughly with clean water. Conditioners help to make the surface of hair smooth, avoiding tangles and making long hair easier to brush.

After washing your hair, let it dry in the air, if you can. If you have long hair, or you are in a hurry, you may have to use a hairdryer. Do not hold it too close or have it too hot, because heat can damage your hair.

WHY DOES MY HEAD ITCH?

Your head can itch for several reasons. You may be using the wrong kind of shampoo, or you may have a flaky **scalp**. This is called dandruff, and it happens when skin flakes because your scalp makes too much oil. You can cure dandruff by using a special shampoo. One other — and the most common — reason for an itchy head is lice.

What are head lice?

Head lice are very small insects that live in people's hair. They feed on tiny amounts of blood from the scalp, and their bites make your head itch. They lay tiny white eggs, called nits, on hairs near the scalp. Nits hatch after about a week. Head lice live for four or five weeks, and they can lay eggs from when they are about two weeks old.

This photo of a head louse has been greatly enlarged. In fact, head lice are only 2–3 millimetres long.

How do you get head lice?

Some people think that you get head lice if your hair is dirty. In fact, head lice prefer clean hair, because it is less greasy for them when they feed. You get head lice from touching heads with someone who already has them. You can also get it by sharing hairbrushes, combs, helmets, hats or scrunchies.

How can you get rid of them?

Some people wash their hair with a special shampoo to kill the head lice. Your whole family should treat their hair at the same time, because the chances are that they have them, too. After you have killed the live lice, you can use a special comb with narrow teeth to comb through the hair and pull out any remaining nits. If you put on a conditioner first, this makes it easier to comb through.

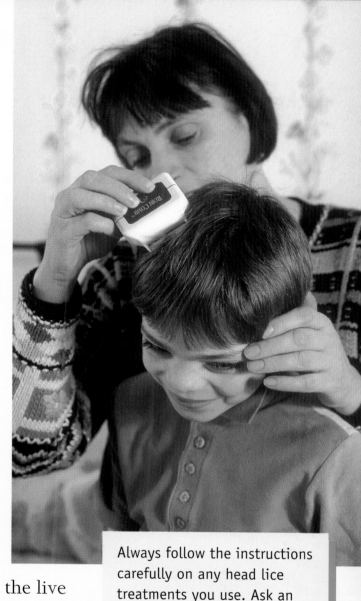

Always follow the instructions carefully on any head lice treatments you use. Ask an adult to help you.

19

WHY SHOULD I BRUSH MY HAIR?

The way you brush your hair and how often you brush it depends on the kind of hair you have. People with short hair may just run a comb through their hair once a day. Long hair gets tangled easily, so it needs brushing more thoroughly with a proper brush.

What does brushing do?

Brushing hair gets rid of some of the dead skin **cells** and dirt that build up in your hair. It also helps to spread the oil produced by the **sebaceous glands** down the whole length your hair. If you have head lice, combing your hair with a fine-toothed comb is an important step in the treatment.

Some people with very curly hair, like this, wear it in braids so that it does not get tangled and does not need brushing!

TOP TIPS FOR BRUSHING YOUR HAIR

- Choose a comb or brush that suits your hair. If you have tight, curly hair, use a wide-toothed comb.

- If you have greasy hair, do not brush too much, because this makes the sebaceous glands produce more oil, which makes your hair even greasier.

- Brush your hair before you wash it, to reduce the number of tangles you get.

- Have your own brush or comb, and try not to share it with anyone else. This avoids spreading **germs** and head lice. Clean your comb or brush regularly.

- When hair is wet, it breaks easily, so try not to brush it until it is dry – or use a wide-toothed comb.

Brush the ends of your hair first, and work your way up. This helps to get any tangles out, and makes it less likely that you will damage your hair.

21

WHY SHOULD I WEAR SUNSCREEN?

Sunlight can damage your hair and your skin. It contains ultraviolet (UV) rays, which are very strong. They can burn your skin and hair, and can also cause a serious disease called skin cancer. On sunny days, you should always wear a hat to shade your hair, and you should wear sunscreen to protect your skin.

People with light skin make less melanin than people with dark skin, so they have to be even more careful in the sun.

Why does my skin darken in the sun?

Have you noticed how your skin gets darker in the sun? This is because the skin tries to protect itself from harmful UV rays, by making more **melanin**. The more melanin your skin makes, the darker your skin looks. You must still use sunscreen even if you have dark skin, but fair-skinned people get sunburnt more quickly.

Which sunscreen should I use?

Every bottle of sunscreen should have the lotion's SPF – Sun Protection Factor – rating. Choose one with an SPF rating of at least 15, which gives you more protection. Rub it all over the uncovered bits of your body, including your ears and feet! Reapply every two or three hours – and more often, if you are swimming or sweating a lot, because this washes it off.

Even if you cover up and wear sunscreen, try to keep out of the sun during the hottest part of the day, between 11 a.m. and 3 p.m.

Other ways to protect your skin

You should also wear T-shirts and shorts or skirts made of tightly woven fabric, which help to block out the sun's rays; a hat with a wide brim, to protect your hair, and the skin on your face and neck; and sunglasses, to protect the delicate skin around your eyes.

WHY DO I GET SPOTS?

Lots of young people get spots as they get older. Spots do not form because you eat too many chips or chocolate bars. Spots form when the **sebaceous glands** in your skin make too much oil.

How do spots form?

Your sebaceous glands make oil to keep the outer layer of skin – the part that is made up of dead **cells** – smooth and supple. Sometimes, these glands make too much oil. When this mixes with dead skin cells, it can form a plug over the **pores** in your skin. White spots form when **bacteria** around a pore get trapped in it. The body makes pus to try to break the bacteria down.

The black bit you can see in a blackhead is not dirt; it is dried oil and skin cells. They turn black because they react with the air.

How can I stop spots?

Everyone gets spots or pimples at some time, and you will not be able to make yourself a pimple-free zone, whatever you do. You can help by cleaning your skin carefully, especially if you have had sunscreen, glitter or face paint on it. Wash your face before you go to bed with a gentle soap and warm water. If your skin does not feel greasy in the morning, just rinse it with warm water. Washing too often with soap can take away the oils that your skin needs.

DON'T PICK ON ME!

The one thing you should not do is to pop or pick a spot. This can make a spot bigger and redder, make it feel sore, and it can damage the delicate skin on your face.

Face paints are fun, but make sure that you wash them off carefully before you go to bed.

WHY HAVE I GOT A SKIN RASH?

A skin rash is when your skin looks red and blotchy. It may feel dry and itchy, too, or the skin may be raised in little blisters.

Lots of different things can cause a skin rash. You may have touched or eaten something that caused it, or sometimes skin rashes happen when you use a different soap or washing-up liquid (if you help with the dishes!). Sometimes, people get a rash after being in the heat, if they touch certain plants or if nettles sting them. Illnesses or some **infections** can also cause rashes. Some people have **allergies** that affect their skin.

Eczema is a skin problem that causes itching and a red rash. It is often caused by a food people eat, or something they breathe in, such as dust. You cannot catch eczema from touching someone who has it.

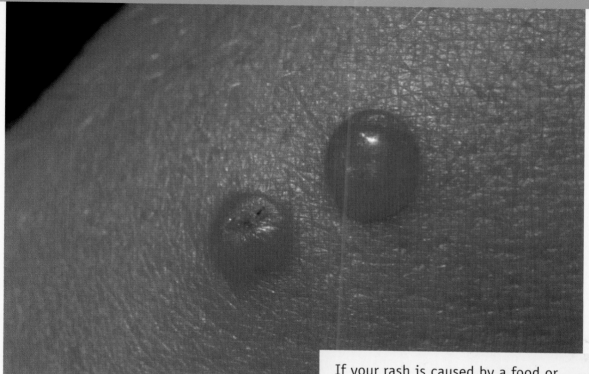

How can I get rid of a rash?

If you get a rash because of something you ate or touched, it should go away by itself quite quickly. If it does not, you should see a doctor. The doctor will give you some medicine to stop the rash. If the rash is caused by an allergy – when your skin reacts badly to something that is usually harmless to other people – a doctor can help you to find out what you are allergic to, and can give you medicine to help.

If your rash is caused by a food or plant, make sure you avoid it in future. These blisters were caused by contact with oil from a poisonous ivy plant.

WHY CAN'T I SCRATCH A RASH?

You should try not to scratch a rash, because this may make your skin red and sore. You can put on camomile lotion or hydrocortisone cream to help to stop that itchy feeling.

27

HOW CAN I SOOTHE SORE SKIN?

Sometimes, your skin can get sore. If you cut yourself, the most important thing to do is to wash the area with soap and warm water. Then put an **antiseptic** cream on, to stop it getting infected. If the cut is big or deep, you may need to see a doctor, who can close up the wound with a special plaster.

How can I soothe sunburn?

Sunburn can feel very sore. Put cool damp flannels on, to lessen the burning feeling. Then soak in a bath of tepid (just warm) water, but do not use soap, because this will make it sorer. Pat yourself dry gently, instead of rubbing your skin. Use an aftersun cream, calamine or aloe lotion, to help to soothe it.

As long as you keep small cuts clean, it is better not to cover them with plasters, because the air will help them to heal. But even larger cuts that need covering do not have to stop you being active.

AMAZING FACTS ABOUT SKIN AND HAIR

- There are about 5 million hairs on a human body, many of them so small that you can barely see them.

- The hairs on your head grow at a rate of about 5 millimetres every week.

- You lose between 50 and 100 hairs from your head every day.

- People with different coloured hair have different numbers of hairs on their head! Redheads have about 80,000 hairs on their head, brown-haired and black-haired people have 100,000, and blondes have at least 120,000.

- When you look at a body, most of what you see is dead! The outer layer of your skin is made of **cells** that died days before.

- You have more hairs on your body than an ape! It is true – but the hair on your body is so short and fine that it is not so obvious.

- You have 7.5 million skin cells on every square centimetre of your body.

GLOSSARY

allergy when the body reacts to something harmless as though it were a germ

antiseptic substance that destroys the germs that cause infections

athlete's foot an infection on the foot

bacteria tiny living things that can cause disease

blood vessels tubes that carry blood in the body

cell the smallest building block of living things

cuticle outer layer of hair

detergents substances that can be used to loosen and remove dirt

epidermis outside layer of the skin

follicle point from which a hair grows

germs tiny living things that can cause disease

gland body part that makes substances, such as sweat

infection when germs get inside the body and cause disease

inherit pass on something from parent to child

keratin kind of hard protein

melanin substance that colours skin and hair

nerve endings these let you feel pain, hot and cold, rough and smooth, and pressure

oxygen gas in the air that we need to breathe

pores tiny holes in the upper layer of your skin

scalp skin and hair that cover the top of the head

sebaceous glands glands under your skin that make a kind of oil, called sebum, that keeps skin and hair soft and waterproof

FURTHER READING

Why Do My Eyes Itch? And Other Questions About Allergies, Angela Royston (Heinemann Library, 2002)

What Does It Mean To Have Allergies? Louise Spilsbury (Heinemann Library, 2001)

INDEX